Take a Look!
Modern Media Literacy

What's the Appeal?

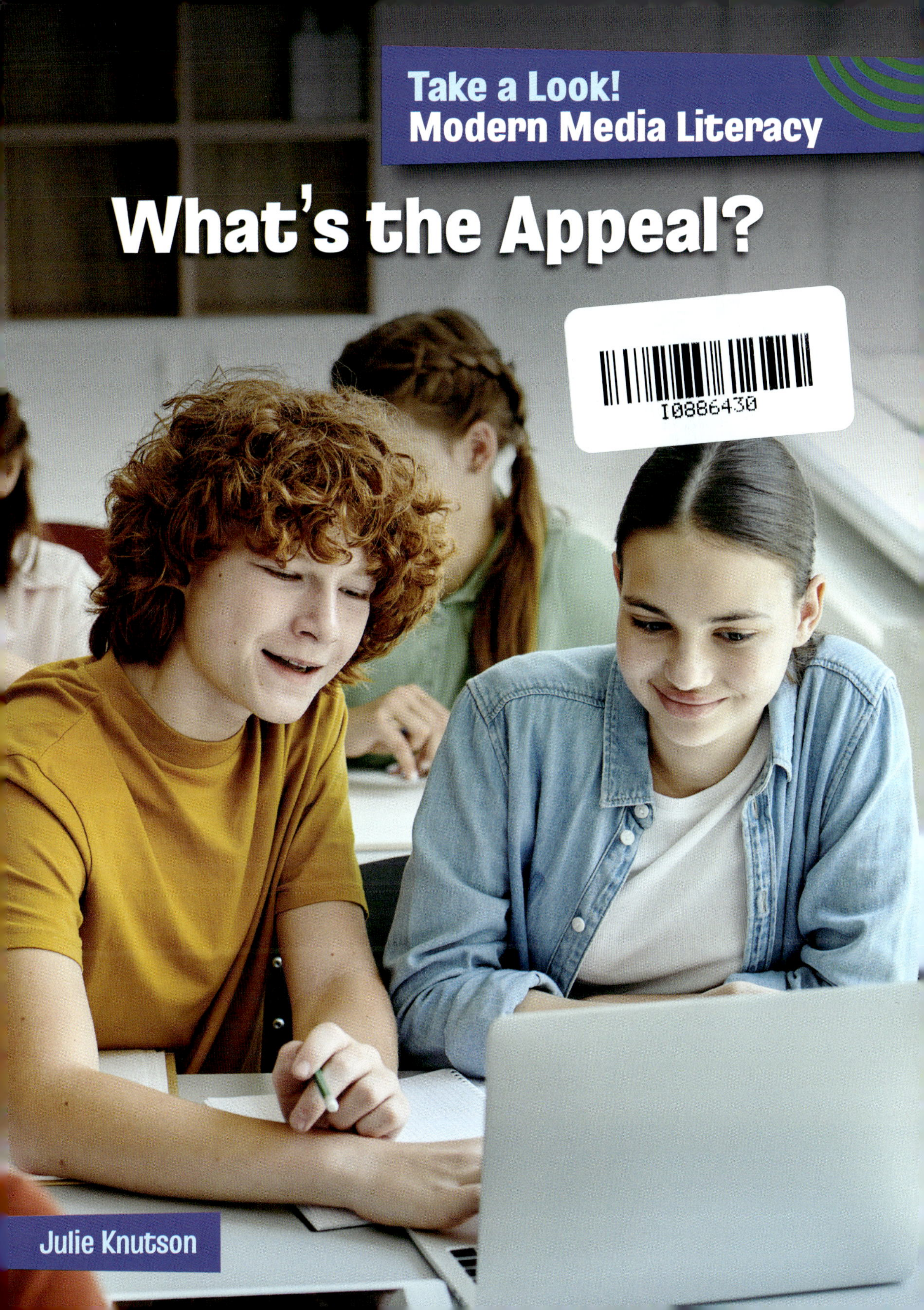

Julie Knutson

CHERRY LAKE PRESS

Published in the United States of America by Cherry Lake Publishing Group
Ann Arbor, Michigan
www.cherrylakepublishing.com

Reading Adviser: Beth Walker Gambro, MS, Ed., Reading Consultant, Yorkville, IL
Content Adviser: Kristin Fontichiaro, Clinical Professor, University of Michigan School of Information

Photo Credits: © LightField Studios/Shutterstock, cover, title page; Smokey Bear image used with the permission of the USDA Forest Service, 5; NPS Photo / Mary Lewandowski, 6; © Lapina/Shutterstock, 7; Jean Leon Gerome Ferris, Public domain, via Wikimedia Commons, 8; © Prostock-studio/Shutterstock, 11; © Clovera/Shutterstock, 12; © aleks333/Shutterstock, 13; © Krakenimages.com/Shutterstock, 15; © PeopleImages.com - Yuri A/Shutterstock 16; © Krakenimages.com/Shutterstock, 17, 18; © LightField Studios/Shutterstock, 19; © AlbertoGandolfo/Shutterstock, 21; © Antonello Marangi/Shutterstock, 22; © Shift Drive/Shutterstock, 23; © Juice Dash/Shutterstock, 25; © SeventyFour/Shutterstock, 26; © Golubovy/Shutterstock, 27; The Ad Council; National Highway Traffic Safety Administration (NHTSA), 28; © PeopleImages.com - Yuri A/Shutterstock, 31

Cherry Lake Press is an imprint of Cherry Lake Publishing Group.

Library of Congress Cataloging-in-Publication Data

Names: Knutson, Julie, author.
Title: What's the appeal? / written by Julie Knutson.
Description: Ann Arbor, Michigan : Cherry Lake Publishing, 2025. | Series: Take a look! Modern media literacy | Audience: Grades 4-6 | Summary: "Part of our Take a Look! Modern Media Literacy series, What's the Appeal? takes a deep dive into the rhetorical appeals that are part of the media we consume, and how readers can utilize this knowledge in their own creation of media. Series closely aligned with standards from the American Association of School Librarians and the Journalism Education Association. This series gives readers a crash course in basic media literacy skills: understanding audience, perspective, persuasive appeals, author's purpose, tracing sources, and creating media content"— Provided by publisher.
Identifiers: LCCN 2024035953 | ISBN 9781668956342 (hardcover) | ISBN 9781668957196 (paperback) | ISBN 9781668958063 (ebook) | ISBN 9781668958933 (pdf)
Subjects: LCSH: Persuasion (Rhetoric) in mass media—Juvenile literature. | Media literacy—Juvenile literature.
Classification: LCC P96.P35 K585 2025 | DDC 302.23—dc23/eng/20240827
LC record available at https://lccn.loc.gov/2024035953

Cherry Lake Press would like to acknowledge the work of the Partnership for 21st Century Learning, a Network of Battelle for Kids. Please visit Battelle for Kids online for more information.

Printed in the United States of America

Note from publisher: Websites change regularly, and their future contents are outside of our control. Supervise children when conducting any recommended online searches for extended learning opportunities.

Julie Knutson (she/her) is an author and educator who lives and works in Philadelphia, PA. She's no stranger to navigating media in our modern world, and she teaches her students to do the same. Whether working with students to craft interview questions or debating designs for a classroom magazine, she also loves guiding middle schoolers through the media-making process.

CONTENTS

Chapter 1:

Take a Look! The Big Picture | 4

Chapter 2:

Break It Down! How Media Makers Create Appeals | 14

Chapter 3:

Show What You Know! Using Rhetorical Appeals | 24

Do More! Extension Activity | 30

Learn More | 31

Glossary | 32

Index | 32

CHAPTER 1

Take a Look! The Big Picture

Eight forest animals huddle in the **foreground** of the poster. They gaze at the viewer with frightened eyes. Smokey Bear stands next to them. He's wearing a park ranger hat, jeans, and a belt. He's holding a shovel. In the background, the sky is deep red. The trees are charred. The critters' home? It's a total wasteland.

A warning message is framed by worried birds, squirrels, deer, and a raccoon: "Another 30 MILLION acres will burn this year—unless *you* are careful! Remember—only *you* can prevent forest fires!"

This poster was created by the U.S. Department of Agriculture (USDA), the Ad Council, and the National Association of State Foresters.

This Smokey Bear poster is from the 1949 Campaign to Prevent Forest, Woods, and Range Fires. It was created by the U.S. Department of Agriculture (USDA), the Ad Council, and the National Association of State Foresters.

The National Park Service seeks to persuade people to care for nature. The next time you read a National Park Service social media post, see if you can spot the logos, pathos, and ethos!

It was a part of a **campaign**. Its designers used very specific techniques to appeal to audiences. The word choices and images draw on three ways of reaching an audience, or **rhetorical appeals**. These appeals are **logos**, **pathos**, and **ethos**. Logos appeals to logic. Pathos appeals to emotion. Ethos appeals to authority. All three are used to persuade people to care for nature.

Animals are often used in media, using pathos, to appeal to emotions. Wouldn't you want to read a post about this puppy?

This drawing of Aristotle by Jean Leon Gerome Ferris (1863–1930) shows him teaching famous leader Alexander the Great. Learning how to persuade an audience was likely an important skill for Alexander the Great.

THINK & COLLABORATE

Look at the poster on page 5 with a peer. What details do you notice? What emotions do the image and words make you feel?

Rhetorical appeals are tools that help **media** makers capture attention and make a point. How can you identify the appeals in messages made to persuade? How do they choose pictures, words, and examples to support their **claims**? Read on to learn more.

Types of Appeals

Rhetorical appeals tap into an audience's values and concerns. The three main pathways for appeal are logos, pathos, and ethos. Often, all three support the author's claim. These ideas have been around for thousands of years. Ancient Greek philosopher Aristotle used them to teach people how a speaker can persuade an audience. All three techniques together are called the **rhetorical triangle**.

BE APPEALS AWARE!

Tricky topic? Activate your "appeals antennae"!

Take **generative artificial intelligence (GenAI)** such as ChatGPT. Many people have strong feelings about students using these technologies. Some claim that schools should teach kids to work responsibly with AI. These folks believe that AI can serve as brainstorming bots or planning buddies. Others disagree. They think AI tools will result in more **plagiarism** and cheating, and students won't learn as much. For this latter group, academic honesty is at stake.

Pause when analyzing the appeals made by people on all sides of the AI argument. Consider their tactics. How are logos, pathos, and ethos used to sway opinion?

LOGOS: What facts support their claim? What's the evidence?

PATHOS: Does the claim spark emotions in a specific audience? How? Why?

ETHOS: Can the person making the claim be trusted? What makes them an expert?

What do you think about GenAI? What rhetorical appeals have you heard or seen people use when arguing about GenAI?

Look again at the forest fire **public service announcement (PSA)**. A PSA is a short ad or ad campaign raising awareness about a public issue. This PSA uses the technique of logos—reasoning with facts and **statistics**—to stress that 30 million acres (12 million hectares) are threatened.

Learning to spot rhetorical appeals is helpful! It gives you more control over the media you see or hear.

THINK & INQUIRE

Have you seen an ad or public service announcement (PSA) recently? What was the point? What appeals do you think the ad makers used?

It also features sad animals that lost their homes. This draws on pathos, which targets emotions. Finally, the campaign uses ethos. An ethos appeal leans into the author's **credibility**. In this PSA, an appeal to ethos is made with Smokey Bear, who is dressed as a park ranger. Park rangers are known wildlife experts. They are respected and trusted authorities. As a result, the audience may trust the ad more.

Identifying appeals is a useful skill. Being able to see how you're being persuaded gives you power. You can choose if you want to engage or not engage with certain media based on what you find.

CHAPTER 2

Break It Down! How Media Makers Create Appeals

Meet Nayeli and Saul!

These friends just learned about logos, pathos, and ethos in English class. They know that knowledge is power! They want to get better at spotting appeals in media.

Nayeli and Saul are also members of the student council. Council members want their school's start time moved to 9 a.m. Nayeli and Saul were asked to talk with the principal about it. They want to do some research first. Then they'll feel more prepared for that talk. This research could also help them practice spotting rhetorical appeals!

Nayeli and Saul want to get good at identifying rhetorical appeals. They want to know how media may be working to persuade them.

They search “changing school start time appeals” online. They find two pieces of media to review. One is a video of a school board meeting. Student speakers were there. The other is a student-written letter to a school board. It was published in a local paper. Nayeli and Saul make a game of spotting appeals in the media they find. First to spot the most appeals wins! They start watching and reading to see what these students had to say.

Nayeli and Saul watch the video. The students at the meeting are arguing for later school start times. They are speaking directly to the school board members. These adults make decisions about local schools.

CREATE & COLLABORATE

Think of a cause you care about. Research by reading and watching diverse perspectives on the cause. What is the most frequently used appeal for this cause? How is the issue presented? Does the media you found grab your attention? How? How does it use colors and/or sound? Work with others to rank the most appealing or convincing sources.

Saul is convinced he'll be able to spot the rhetorical appeals fastest! Let's see who wins.

Nayeli and Saul start to spot appeals. They're thinking through logos, pathos, and ethos. Which will they spot first?

The first student speaker begins:
"Is the 6 hours of sleep a night that many students at our middle school get enough? According to experts: "NO." Scientists at the Centers for Disease Control and Prevention (CDC) state that sleep is critical for teen health. Because of this, experts say that the school day shouldn't begin before 8:30 a.m." "That's logos and ethos!" Nayeli and Saul yell at the same time. Guess this one's a tie. The student speaker is appealing to logic through the use of facts. The CDC is an authority, so that appeal is also definitely ethos.

The next student speaker steps up to the podium. She begins:
"Middle schoolers are experts when it comes to our schedules. We live through them every day! If we are active in many extracurriculars, we may not get home until 9 p.m. By the time homework is done and we get to bed, it could be midnight. The next morning, we may wake up at 6 a.m. Then we get only 6 hours of sleep—3 full hours less than the minimum suggested by the CDC! We barely have time to dream."

Nayeli and Saul agree. "That's pathos!" exclaims Nayeli. The speaker used pathos by stating that students barely had time to dream. Poor students! Emotional appeal, for sure. "There's also ethos AND logos!" says Saul. By using a CDC fact, the speaker appealed to people's trust in authority. The timeline? That appealed to logic. Nayeli and Saul are still tied.

They pull up the letter in the newspaper. Nayeli and Saul start reading. The author, a student, has many of the same feelings they do. The author states, *"Oftentimes, teachers say that we are tired and unfocused in the morning. These charges leave us hurt and powerless. Why? If we could, we'd sleep in! Then we'd come to school refreshed and ready to learn. Please push back the start of the school day, just by an hour."* "Pathos!" yells Nayeli, right as Saul starts saying the same. This writer's appeal to emotion was clear. That's a win for Nayeli!

Nayeli and Saul think the students considered their audience well. They assumed the school board cared about learning. They assumed they cared about child development and well-being. Nayeli and Saul remember that creators always need to think of their audience. If creators think through what their audience cares about, they can craft stronger appeals.

EXPERT SPOTLIGHT: CLIMATE ACTIVIST GRETA THUNBERG

Greta Thunberg regularly delivers strong appeals to global leaders. Her speeches and writings blend logos, pathos, and ethos to demand climate action. Read this short **excerpt** from her 2019 speech to the United Nations (UN). Where in her speech do you spot ethos, pathos, and logos?

"This is all wrong. I shouldn't be up here. I should be back in school on the other side of the ocean. Yet you all come to us young people for hope. How dare you!

For more than 30 years, the science has been crystal clear. How dare you continue to look away and come here saying that you're doing enough, when the politics and solutions needed are still nowhere in sight.

You say you hear us and that you understand the urgency. But no matter how sad and angry I am, I do not want to believe that. Because if you really understood the situation and still kept on failing to act, then you would be evil. And that I refuse to believe."

Greta Thunberg began her climate activism career at age 15. She is well known for launching the School Strike for Climate, in which she led protests to demand environmental action.

Nayeli and Saul know they should still find some more sources. They want to find some other viewpoints. They know there will likely be some adults against later start times. They think these viewpoints will help them have a better understanding of the issue. But they're well on their way to being more informed. They're happy they were able to spot the rhetorical appeals in these arguments. It helped them feel more aware of the media they were taking in.

CHAPTER 3

Show What You Know! Using Rhetorical Appeals

You know the three types of rhetorical appeals. The strongest appeals use all three. You can see them at work in media all around you. You can also use logos, pathos, and ethos to support your own claims. Use these core steps for crafting strong appeals:

- **Choose a Topic:** Identify something that you feel strongly about. Maybe it's screen time. Maybe it's school lunch or the value of video games. This will help you know what words or images to use.

- **State Your Claim:** What claim are you making? What do you want your audience to do or believe?

It's always important to think about your audience before crafting an appeal. One kind of appeal may work better than another.

Even if you'll be filming a video or giving a speech, it's helpful to write out what you're planning to say. This will help you get your rhetorical appeals just right!

- **Build Your Logic:** Gather facts. Find definitions. Identify cause and effect relationships. Build ideas on each other. Start simple. Build up to your conclusion.

- **Identify an Authority:** Experts and expert opinions go a long way. Find out what the experts think. Look for articles or videos by experts or interviewing experts. Include quotes and research results that support your claim.

- **Choose an Emotional Appeal:** What emotion are you hoping to create in your audience? Fear? Joy? A feeling of community and belonging? How you want your audience to feel about your claim, or the consequences of not agreeing with you, can guide the images, colors, and even sounds that you use.

You now have the tools to both spot appeals and make your own. Use this knowledge wisely!

THINK & CURATE

Write an opinion piece for your school newspaper using logos. How will you find good sources of information for appealing to logos? What questions will you ask to decide if a source is worth using?

The right appeal in media grabs the attention of the audience. It makes them care. It could even save lives!

APPEALS ALL AROUND US!

The Red Cross. The USDA. The White House. For more than 80 years, the Ad Council has partnered with these groups and many more! It's produced campaigns on topics ranging from COVID-19 vaccines to racial justice to mental health.

In 1941, ad executive James Webb Young decided that his industry should do more for the social good. He established the Ad Council to "educate, unite, and uplift."

What's the secret of the Ad Council's success? Rhetorical appeals. Consider their campaign to prevent distracted driving. The campaign's goal is to convince drivers to keep their eyes on the road instead of on their devices.

In one video, a man is watching a shark video on his phone as he drives. When he looks up, he has to slam on the brakes. His car screeches to a halt. He almost hit a woman in a crosswalk! She looks terrified but unharmed. One of the final frames shows his phone in his cupholder. The message flashes: "Eyes forward. Don't drive distracted." The goal of this video was to make people feel something! The ad makers appealed to emotion with pathos.

Do More!

Extension Activity

We opened this book by analyzing a PSA. Keep in mind the information presented in this book and make your own PSA. Remember, a PSA is supposed to raise public knowledge of a specific issue. Think of an issue you care about. Does the issue affect other kids your age? Neighbors? Your family? Think through what you feel passionate about. Then get to work.

As you do so, keep the points from Chapter 3 in mind:

- **Choose a Topic**
- **State Your Claim**
- **Know Your Audience**
- **Build Your Logic**
- **Identify an Authority**
- **Choose an Emotional Appeal**

These steps will help you say what you need to say. Now decide how you want to share it. Hang your posters around school? Post your video to social media? Publish your cartoon in the school paper? Sharing ideas is the point of media, so get out there and share responsibly!

Learn More

Book

Down, Susan Brophy. *Power and Persuasion in Media and Advertising.* New York, NY: Crabtree, 2018.

On the Web

Search these online sources with an adult:

- Read, Write, Think—The Art of Rhetoric | video
- Thesaurus.com—Understand the Difference Between Ethos, Pathos, and Logos to Make Your Point

Glossary

campaign (kam-PAYN) a series of actions performed to reach a specific goal

claims (KLAYMZ) main ideas an author tries to prove in an argument

credibility (kreh-duh-BIH-luh-tee) trustworthiness

ethos (EE-thahs) appeal based on the credibility or character of the author, tapping into the audience's sense of ethics

excerpt (EK-serpt) a short selection from a larger work

foreground (FOR-grownd) toward the front of an image

generative artificial intelligence (JEH-nuh-ruh-tive ar-tuh-FIH-shuhl in-TEH-luh-juhns) computer programs that input data from sources on the internet and then output different combinations of that data

logos (LOH-guhs) appeal based on facts and numbers, tapping into the audience's logic

media (MEE-dee-uh) the means of communicating information to large numbers of people, including television, newspapers, magazines, and radio

pathos (PAY-thohs) appeal based on emotion, tapping into the audience's feelings and senses

plagiarism (PLAY-juh-rih-zuhm) the act of claiming another person's work as your own

public service announcement (PUH-blik SER-vuhs uh-NOWN-smuhnt) a short advertisement raising awareness about a public issue; often sponsored by the government or a non-profit group

rhetorical appeals (rih-TOR-ih-kuhl uh-PEELZ) qualities of an argument that persuade people to support it

rhetorical triangle (rih-TOR-ih-kuhl TRIE-ain-guhl) a name for all three rhetorical appeals as one group

Index

academic integrity, 10
activities, 30
Ad Council, 4–5, 29
advertising, public service, 4–6, 11, 13, 28–30
Aristotle, 8–9
artificial intelligence (AI), 10–11
audience messaging, 6, 9, 20, 24–25, 27, 30

climate activism, 21–22
credibility appeals, 6, 9–10, 13, 19–20

emotional appeals, 6–7, 9–10, 13, 20, 28–29

ethics issues, AI, 10
ethos (rhetorical appeal), 6, 9–10, 13, 19–20

fact-based appeals, 6, 9–11, 19–20, 27

logos (rhetorical appeal), 6, 9–11, 19–20, 27

media formats, 27, 30
media literacy
  benefits, 12–13
  spotting rhetorical appeals, 9–12, 14–21, 23

pathos (rhetorical appeal), 6–7, 9–10, 13, 20, 28–29

plagiarism, 10
posters (media), 4–5, 9, 30
public service advertising, 4–6, 11, 13, 28–30

research, in appeals creation, 14, 16, 19–20, 23, 27, 30
rhetorical appeals
  crafting, 24–27, 30
  defined and described, 6–7, 9–13, 16, 19–21, 27–29
  importance, 8–9, 11, 21, 28–29
  spotting, 9–12, 14–21, 23

Thunberg, Greta, 21–22